Ramblings of My Heart

Arunima Guha Roy

BookLeaf Publishing

India | USA | UK

Presentation by *BookLeaf Publishing*

Web: www.bookleafpub.com

E-mail: info@bookleafpub.com

ISBN: 9789363315143

First edition 2024

To my daughter, Kiara,

"I'll protect you until the end of time,

so that you will never lose yourself."

ACKNOWLEDGEMENT

To everyone who has directly and indirectly made a mark in my life, whose journey has deeply affected me into shaping the person I am today.

To my parents, my partner, my close friends, and my fictional characters.

PREFACE

This book of poems takes you on a journey through the life of a person who might have had similar experiences like you, shares your opinions, your feelings, and is telling you that you are not alone, you are not lonely. You enjoy solitude. You might not connect with everyone around you, but there is someone exactly like you breathing the same air, seeing the same star and the moon, or even laying down on a bed and looking at their ceiling, thinking about the same things as you.

Shadows in the Night

A house full of people,
A mind full of thoughts.
A world full of opportunities,
But the heart thinks of none.
For every day feels like the same night,
Filled with the same thought:
Despair. Loneliness.
Unfulfilled dreams.
Roads not taken.

And the mind searches for that light,
That one chance to make everything alright.
Ready to juggle life and compromise,
In a way that seems fine.

Travelling in Dimensions

Travel with your eyes,
Travel with your heart.
Travel to search for who you really are.
'Cause they say
That a cat has nine lives,
But you have just one.
Whether you believe in words or art,
Or you believe in walking your own path.

Travel to find different people like you—
To learn, to grow, or just to breathe.
Travel to experience, travel to relax,
To find yourself among the rest.

Did I just...

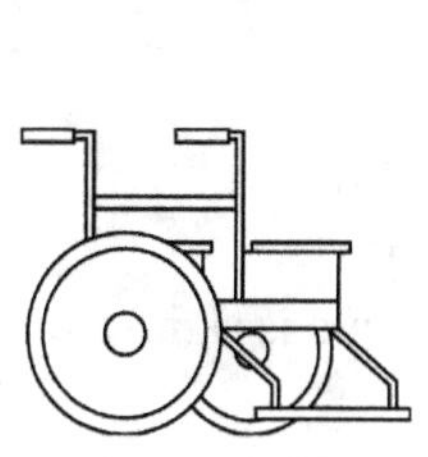

Did I just do what I did?
Did I just say what I said?
Is it just me, or everyone else?
Thinking, observing,
Drowning in self-doubt.

What would I be, if not this?
What would I have done, if not that?
Where would I go, if not here?
Where would this end, if not now?

The challenge seems hard at first;
The struggle and pain feel constant.
So many questions occupy my mind—
When will I learn that
There is never a specific time?

For time is overrated.
'Now or never' is for deadlines.

Things happen when they happen,
And we are not in control.
Sometimes the right time
Is simply when you can—
When it feels right.
So just do it.
Do it because you feel ready,
Do it 'cause it needs to be done.
But do it in a way you believe is right.

If not now, you'll eventually find your way.
'Cause that's what happens in life, doesn't it?

Because It Is Your First Time

When someone comes into your life,
They come with their experiences,
Their whole life.

Be it good or bad,
They come with their fragile heart—
Hearts full of baggage,
Hearts full of expectations.

But there is hope.
There should be hope.

For what you've experienced before
Is different when you do it
With someone new.

Because it is your first time—
The first time for both of you.

Love is different.

For you loved him
Because of who he was,
For how he made you feel.
When you loved him,
You didn't know the feeling before him.

Now, when you love,
You know you've fallen in love
For how he makes you feel.

And both are different.

Because it is your first time—
The first time for both of you.

Now your fragile hearts are together,
Learning to take care of each other.

Failing, or a Failure?

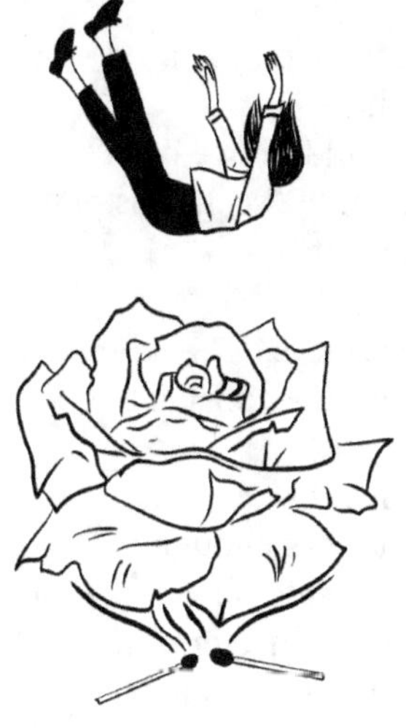

There is a difference between failing
and being a failure.

You can only be a failure if you give up.

So don't let your spirits go down,
and don't give up.
'Cause one day it will all fall into place.
It always does.

What could I have been?

Sometimes I wonder,
If I were not here,
Where else would I have been?
I think about all the scenarios in my head.
Playing on repeat,
Amidst a new set of chaos,
With different faces,
And some with my constants.

When will I feel
That what I have is enough?
That I am blessed to be where I am?
I had imagined a different life—
But do we really get to choose
The life we want to live?

Even if you try hard,
Even if you make changes—
To the routine,
To the setting,
To ourselves—
Does it really get better?
Will I ever be able to be where I want to be?

Love Yourself First

No, you're not asking for too much.
You are just asking the wrong person.
Don't waste your energy
On those who don't value you.

You deserve to be loved and cherished.
And when someone can't see that,
it's their loss, not yours.
So, love yourself first.

What matters is you

You don't need big dreams.
You need something that matters to you.

And when you find that,
No matter what anybody says or does
You will stand tall through it all.

Because It Is My First Love

I fell in love with his warm heart,
His emotional gaze,
The feeling when he held my hand—
Warm and comfortable.

For how he said, "Where was I this whole time?"
For how he regretted not meeting me sooner.
For when he always sees to it that I'm safe,
For when he checks if I am doing okay.
For when his eyes well up with love,
With emotions and pride.
For when his heart beats for me,
And shows me how much I mean to him.
For when his hugs keep me warm—
So comfortable that I feel at home.

For when I know he is all mine,
All mine to keep.

I love him with all my heart,
Because he gave me his,
Because he shows me what love is,
Because he makes me feel cherished,
Because he makes me feel his.

Because it is my first time,
Knowing this feeling,
Knowing something so pure,
Knowing that I belong.

I belong to someone with a pure heart,
A heart that beats for me,
A heart that shares my feelings—

Because it is my first love,
The love that is all mine to keep.

Furnace

I told you,
To treat everyone like a furnace—
To stay close enough,
But not too close.

If you're afraid that your heart will break,
And you won't recover from it,
Even though sometimes you can't help it,
Even though you want it all—

There is nothing wrong
In protecting yourself first.

For it's only you,
Only you who can take care of your heart.

Stay close enough,
But not too close.

For you're not lonely,
For you're not wrong—
But it's your heart.

For it's only you,
Only you who can take care of it.

Treat everyone like a furnace—
Stay close enough,
But not too close,
Like I told you so.

Childhood

When all you craved
was love, attention, and chocolates,
When your world revolved around
a game of tag with your friends,
Cuddles from your grandparents,
and treats from your parents.

When you were
the centre of attention for your folks,
And they took pride
in displaying your talents to family and friends.
When everything around you
seemed happy and bright,
And you lived a carefree life,
dreaming of starry nights and fairy tales.

Hide and Seek

Just like the sunrays
Dancing through palm leaves,
Playing hide and seek,
Caressing your olive skin in spring,
With a heart brimming with dreams
Of what's to come.

I look forward to a starry night
And a gleaming moon,
Shining over a restless sea,
In windy winters,
Lost in thoughts of days gone by.

Listen

Listen,
When there's a cry for help.
You never know when things might end,
While you were busy assuming
Everything was okay.

Speak Out

Experiences lead to stories,
But only some make it to the headlines.

Blank Space

Sometimes, when you've been through a lot
emotionally,
Your heart and mind go blank.
Perhaps a way to cope,
Perhaps to give yourself a break,
Perhaps to prevent getting carried away with
frustration,
And hurting yourself further.

The Lonely Soul

There are many who want
to talk about themselves,
Who want to be asked how they are doing,
Who want to speak about the things
that have been worrying them,
Who want to share incidents
From their lives that hold meaning.
They aren't looking for reasons;
They aren't looking for advice or solutions.

All they want is to talk about themselves.

But sometimes, no one asks,
While some only ask
to give unsolicited advice
Or pass judgements.

And that is not okay.

This need for attention is not selfish.
They seek attention because they are lonely
And are in need of some company.

So lend your ear if you can,
Not to pass judgement
Or to give advice and solutions.
You never know,
They might just inspire you with their stories,
Or their stories might help you face
Or overcome that thing you have been avoiding.

What is Love?

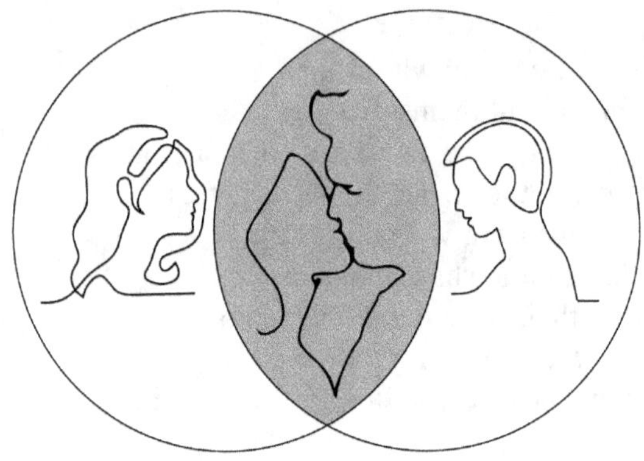

Is it when two people meet
And fall in love with each other?
Or when two people who are in love
Come together?

Everything's Gonna Be Okay

Your tears are falling,
Your heart is in pain.
Time seems to drag on,
But eventually, it's all gonna be okay.

Drops of Survival

You don't cry because you are weak;
You cry because you want to survive.

Alone

Sometimes, I feel so utterly alone.
I learned long ago that we're born alone
And will die alone.
But now, the thought lingers—
will I be left with no one?
No one to share my life,
My stories, my troubles, my laughter.
No one to understand my thoughts,
To join me on trips I long to take.

I wonder what will happen
When my parents are no longer here.
Who will I turn to?
Who will be there to share my world?
Time has changed all of us;
Responsibilities and distance
Have pulled us apart.
We're no longer the simple souls we used to be.
Every relationship feels different now,
And I feel myself drifting,
As though no one is truly by my side.

Everyone is moving on,
Finding new connections,
While I fear I'll be left without family,
Without friends.
It's hard to form new bonds,
I no longer have the energy to start fresh—
To introduce myself, to build something new.

I want the people in my life today
To stay with me until my last day,
Just as I wish to be a part of theirs.
Why is it so hard to find your people?
To hold onto those who feel like home?
I worry that I'll be left without a place to belong,
That I'll have no family,
no friends to call my own. I cherish solitude,
But loneliness frightens me.

Drifting Friendships

Friends are slipping out of touch.
Even when I reach out, it's not like before.
It aches my heart to think
Of all the moments we shared—
I crave the closeness, the effortless bond we had.

I know time and distance have changed things,
And life has taken us down different paths,
But still, I miss the friendship we once knew.
It saddens me how easily it fades away.

Why is it so hard to stay connected?
Why do replies take so long,
And making time for each other
Feels like a distant memory?

We're all drifting apart,
And it fills me with sadness.
Yes, when we do reconnect,
It feels like the old days,
But those moments are fleeting,
And the distance returns.

I wish we could stay close,
That life hadn't placed this space between us.
The struggles we face
Make it harder to reach out.

Is it that they no longer want me in their lives?
I'll never truly know.

Friendship

Friends come in all sizes—
In groups of five or just one,
From the neighbourhood, the workplace,
College halls, and school days—
Some across cities and miles,
Each knowing a different side of you.

Distance and time may test us,
But when we meet, it feels as if
Time has stood still.
They bring out the best and worst,
Lending an ear, grounding you,
Cheering through ups and downs.

When they're absent, you miss their laughter,
Recall the moments shared—
Cracking up or shedding tears

Over old stories that bind you.

Friends are vital—sometimes more than family;
True friends don't care for your past,
They see you for who you are,
Accepting, annoying, confiding,
Loving you unconditionally.

They ease your mind in tough times,
And though distance may pull you apart,
When you reunite, you fall back into place,
Becoming the person you were with them.
What a privilege, what joy
To find friendships that hold your heart
As if it were their own.
Sometimes friends feel like family;
Often, they mean even more.

To My Parents

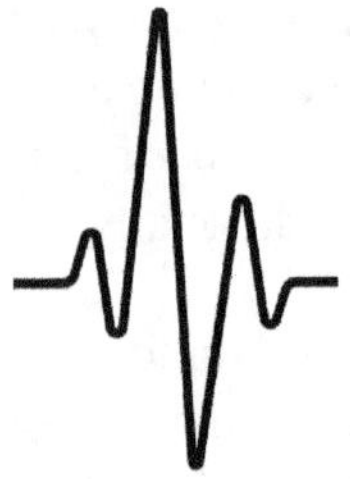

In quiet moments, I reflect,
On all the love you've given,
The lessons taught, the paths you've paved,
The sacrifices made, the dreams you've driven.

Through sleepless nights and worry lines,
You held my hand and guided me,
In laughter's glow and sorrow's shade,
You showed me strength and set me free.

With every hug and every cheer,
You built a home where hope could grow,
In every story, every tear,
You taught me more than you could know.

You celebrated my every win,
And caught my falls with open arms,
You taught me kindness, patience, grace,
And how to navigate life's storms.

Though time may change and paths may part,
Your wisdom echoes in my heart.
No distance can diminish the bond—
The love you gave, the light you sparked.

Even as I've grown and faced my fears,
Your lessons guide me through the years.
The path you paved still lights my way,
Your voices linger, come what may.

I recall the times we spent as one,
Moments etched, like rays of the sun.
I navigate my issues now,
With every memory, I take a bow.

No one in the world knows me completely—
No one else I'd share my life with so sweetly.
Sometimes I wonder what I'd do,
In a world without the love of you.

So here's to you, my guiding stars,
The roots that ground, the wings that soar.
With gratitude that knows no end,
I cherish you forevermore.

To My Daughter

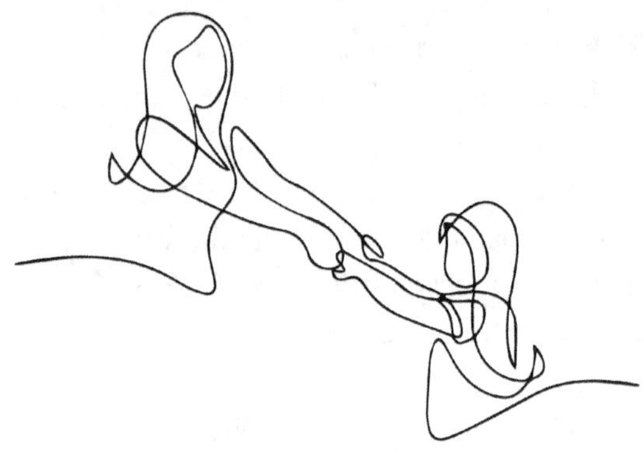

You are the sunshine that lights up my world.
The sound of your giggles
Fills my heart with warmth,
Bringing me happiness,
Words just can't describe.
Your tiny hands, your tiny feet—
Forever mine to hold and cherish.

You're the little star in my life,
Who understands me so much,
Even though you're so small.
You listen, you look up to me,
And I can only hope
To guide you, to always be there by your side.

I want to help you become strong,
Confident, and independent,
Ready to face any challenge
That comes your way.

I'm so proud when I see you
Doing things all by yourself,
Thinking, remembering, and figuring things out,
Even at such a young age.

You're already so wise beyond your years,
And I hope I can be part of the magic
That makes your life wonderful.
Seeing you up on stage, dancing so perfectly
At just three or four—
It made my heart burst with pride,
That I couldn't control my tears.

Sometimes, I wonder how I got so lucky
To have you in my life.
With you, I've grown as a person,
And I know we'll keep growing together.
You make me feel both strong
And vulnerable at the same time,
And I will protect you
With everything I have, always.

I might stumble,
But I promise I'll always try harder for you.
Without you, I don't know how
I would've gotten through the challenges
That made me who I am today.

So, let's keep growing together, my love—
Side by side, always.

A Reminder to Myself

I am strong-willed, with talents untold,
Bold in spirit, and confident, never cold.
I need to be stronger, to stand my ground,
For in life's storms, my strength is found.

I've faced many trials, learned lessons anew,
And keenly observed all that life threw.
I reflect on the past, think deeply each day,
Pushing forward in every possible way.

I try hard each moment, and harder I'll try,
With faith in myself, I will reach the sky.
I won't let setbacks steal my fight,
For I know my worth, and I know my light.

Though luck may not favour me, I stand tall,
I alone can break through every wall.
More confidence, more faith, is what I need,
To believe in the greatness I'm destined to lead.

Yes, I am kind and sometimes naive,
But I won't let heartache make me grieve.
Though I feel deeply and take things to heart,
I know in my soul, I'll never fall apart.

I'll rise above each problem I face,
For nothing can stop me in this race.
I will reach each height I set my mind to,
And take care of myself, body and soul too.

I am strong, and I will always believe—
In myself, in the life I know I'll achieve.

Journey of Reflection

I love to travel;
It reveals how small I am
In this vast, swirling world.

I reflect on my journey—
Who I've been,
What I've done,
The lessons learned
That have shaped me.

I watch the people,
The landscapes shifting,
And realise my place
Is but a whisper
In this grand universe,
A reminder that there's so much
To learn, to grow, to explore.

In these moments,
I forget all sorrow;
I feel free—
Losing myself in the world around me.
Even in company, I hardly speak,
Not from upset or unfriendliness,
But from surrendering to the journey.

I let go,
My mind mostly empty,
Grasping everything I see,
Everything I feel.
I feel liberated,
Rejuvenated,
Discovering a new sense of purpose,
A fresh sense of being.